How to Plan Small Projects

What You Need To Do Before You Start

Geoff Higgins

A Word template using the approach in this book is available at
www.performancepeople.com.au
under Resources > How to Plan Small Projects.

How to Plan Small Projects

Published by Performance People Pty Ltd
www.performancepeople.com.au

© Copyright 2010 Performance People Pty Ltd.
All rights reserved. No part of this book may be reproduced or utilised in any form or by any means, electronic or mechanical, including photocopying, scanning or other analogue or digital recording, without permission in writing from the publisher, except for brief quotations appropriately attributed.

ISBN 978-0-9808631-0-9

Table of Contents

Table of Contents	iv
Glossary	v
Useful Resources	vi
1. Introduction	**1**
1.1 Being a Project Manager	1
2. What is a Project?	**2**
3. The 7 Ps	**4**
4. Project Information	**6**
5. The Project Definition (Applying the 7 P's)	**8**
5.1 The Project Name	9
5.2 The Project Objective(s)	10
5.3 The Project Client	13
5.4 Project Activities	15
5.5 Project Team	16
5.6 Project Budget	18
5.7 Project End	20
5.8 The Project Name (again)	20
6. The Project Schedule	**21**
A Template for a Project Schedule	22
6.1 Create the Project Schedule	23
6.2 Enough or More Needed?	24
7. A More Comprehensive Project Definition	**25**
7.1 Project Monitoring & Reporting	26
7.2 Organisational Commitment & Capacity	28
7.3 Stakeholder Analysis	29
7.4 Project Location	30
7.5 Securing & Keeping Resources	31
7.6 Project Risks & Issues	32
7.7 Are You Finished Yet?	33
Project Plan Template	**34**
8. Endnote: An Explanation	**39**
Acknowledgements	**40**

Glossary

Deliverables	Tangible things that will be created or achieved during or by the end of the project. (Also known as 'project outputs'.)
Duration	The amount of time something will take to happen. (Also known as 'elapsed time'.)
Issue	An actual project problem.
Milestone	Something that occurs during the life of the project which is important and does not involve work effort or a duration.
Project	Something that is complex enough to need to be planned, and solves a problem; enables you to seize an opportunity; and/or changes your world in some way.
Project Definition	A detailed plan of the project.
Project End	The date when the project must, should and/or will finish.
Project Plan	The Project Definition and Project Schedule put together (and preferably signed off by the client).
Risk	A potential project problem.
Schedule	A timeline of project activity, including milestones, work effort and resources.
Scope	The set of deliverables of the project. (Also, the things that will not be delivered are 'out of scope'.)
Work (Effort)	Time expended doing something. This is the same as the old-fashioned term 'man hours'.

Useful Resources

Books

37signals et al. 2009, *Getting Real: The smarter, faster, easier way to build a successful web application*, 37signals (self-published at www.lulu.com)

Baker, S & Baker, K 1998, *The Complete Idiot's Guide to Project Management*, Alpha Books.
(4th edition published 2007.)

DeMarco, T 1997, *The Deadline, A Novel About Project Management*, Dorset House.

Manas, J 2006, *Napoleon on Project Management: Timeless Lessons in Planning, Execution, and Leadership*, Thomas Nelson.

Websites

www.performance-people.com.au/Resources/Res_Project.html
Performance People Pty Ltd Project Management & Microsoft Project Resources

www.pmi.org   The USA Project Management Institute.

www.gantthead.com   An online community for PMs – lots of useful articles & forums.

www.fastcompany.com   Search for project management stories about real organisations.

Blogs

www.reformingprojectmanagement.com by Hal McComber

Podcasts

Jerry Manas: Project Results Podcast
(not being updated, but an excellent resource)

Cornelius Fichtner: The Project Management Podcast

1. Introduction

There are a small number of critical principles in managing projects, and a large number of accepted practices. This book presents as many of the principles and accepted practices as I can cram in. It is intentionally light on theory and heavy on basics which should enable you to be successful.

A good plan is your best way to avoid trouble as a project manager. Staying out of trouble is often about good decision making – knowing when to stick to the plan, and when to ignore it.

Good project managers are 'on top of' their project. Sound planning is the ladder you climb to get there.

1.1 Being a Project Manager

You can be a very good project manager if you do the things in this book consistently and creatively. Consistently follow the principles and apply the practices, and apply your creativity to improve on them.

To benefit most from this book, you should apply what you are reading about to an actual project. At the end of most topics there is a section called 'Activity' which will reinforce what you are learning.

2. What is a Project?

A great way to determine whether something is a project is to ask:
Am I likely to forget something or stuff it up if I am careless?

If the answer is 'yes', I feel the need to plan it out and act like it is a project. Different people will have a different level of capacity to 'just get things done', so this does not result in a clear distinction between projects and other activities.

Some other perspectives on 'what is a project?' are:
It solves a problem.
It enables you to seize an opportunity.
It changes your world in some way.

In a business context, the overall goal can be described as the venture or the vision (depending how practical or visionary you are). This is generally something really big, like building the Sydney Opera House. The project could be selecting a design or installing the guttering (of the Opera House). Again, this does not result in a clear distinction between projects and other activities, but it is a handy approach.

Identifying a project can be tricky. It is a slippery concept, and you may have a difference of opinion on it at times.

Ultimately a project is what you call a project. If it is spring cleaning, that's fine. If it is renovating an old house, that is fine too. If it is building the Sydney Opera House, great, but you may be reading the wrong book. This book is about small projects.

How to Plan Small Projects

A rose by any other name…

If people around you (or you yourself) are uncomfortable with the term 'project', don't be deterred. There are lots of names for projects, including:
- Initiative
- Activity
- Undertaking
- Assignation
- Happening
- Scheme
- Mission (thanks to the Blues Brothers movie).

And specialised terms, like:
- Event
- Expedition
- Assignment
- Road trip
- Conference
- Workshop
- Session
- Office move
- Construction
- Barn raising
- And more.

If you or others are uncomfortable (or bored) with the term 'project', be creative.

3. The 7 Ps

The 7 Ps is one of the 'critical principles' mentioned in the Introduction. It is simply a reminder that you MUST get some key things done before the project starts properly.

My friend Michael Plant introduced me to the concept of the 7 Ps more than 15 years ago. Often people ask me how they got in the mess they find themselves in. And I tell them about the 7 Ps.

(Caution, minor expletive follows.) The 7 Ps are:

Prior Preparation and Planning Prevents Piss-Poor Performance.

For those of you of a sensitive persuasion, you can drop the fifth word, and the point can still be made with 6 Ps.

Nike might exhort you to 'Just do it!', but if you do, you might do things you didn't need to do, or in the wrong order. If you take the time to plan before taking action, you have a better chance of figuring out what you need to do, how you will do it, who will be involved, and make other important decisions.

Planning a project involves asking a series of questions. By asking these questions each time, planning should become second nature.

At a minimum, answer:

1. What to call the project?
2. What do I want to achieve?
3. Why am I doing this?
4. Who am I doing it for?
5. How am I going to start?
6. What will I do along the way?
7. How am I going to finish?
8. Who else will be doing the project?
9. What should the project cost?
10. How soon do I need to/expect to finish?

I have used the word 'I' in the list above, not 'we', because many small projects are an individual undertaking. If you are working with others in a collaborative manner, substitute 'we'.

Don't worry about answering these yet. The rest of this book is about answering these questions, and some other ones too, like:

11. How am I going to keep track and how will I report project status?
12. Does my organisation have the will and the capacity, to complete the project?
13. Who is important to the project, and why?
14. Where will the project be undertaken, and where is the best place/space?
15. How can the resources be secured by the project? (Resources include cash, people and other things.)
16. What are the known risks and issues, and how will I address them?

Serious project managers may call the resulting information a Project Definition, Project Plan or Project Specification.

4. Project Information

The effective project manager quickly becomes a clearinghouse of important and trivial project information. To be that clearinghouse, first the project manager must absorb a huge amount of information about the project. Even small projects can potentially involve large amounts of information.

Some suggested questions you need to answer as soon as possible after taking on the role of project manager include:
- How will I measure success (in quantity and quality)?
- What else could be achieved that may be beneficial?
- What could go wrong during the project?
- Will all of the outcomes be positive?
- What processes should I follow?
- What safety criteria should I consider?
- What impact could this have on other parts of my organisation?
- What machinery and tools are required?
- Are there any issues obtaining the machinery and tools?
- Do people need to be released from other duties?
- Who needs to know about the project?
- How much do they need to know?
- Will any downtime impact on the project?
- How much will the project cost?
- What are the consequences of project failure (for the organisation, the stakeholders, the project team and the project manager)?

Organising this information can be challenging.

How to Plan Small Projects

If you like mind-maps, this is a great way to organise large amounts of information. If you are a notebook kind of person, get a notebook ASAP and write the project name on the front. Number the notebook "1", as you may need more than one.

Some of this information will go into your Project Definition, the rest of it may never be useful, but you just never know, and if you do need it, chances are you will be able to find it – if you are organised.

How to Plan Small Projects

5. The Project Definition (Applying the 7 P's)

The Project Definition will consist of the following content. The right column gives the relevant project management jargon.

At a minimum, you need to know:

1. What to call the project?	Project Name
2. What do I want to achieve? 3. Why am I doing this?	Project Objective
4. Who am I doing it for?	Project Client
5. How am I going to start? 6. What will I do along the way? 7. How am I going to finish?	Project Activities
8. Who else will be doing the project?	Project Team
9. What should the project cost?	Project Budget
10. How soon do I need to/expect to finish?	Project End

5.1 The Project Name

A project should have a name that is short, relevant and novel. You will appreciate having kept it short when you type it for the 15,000th time. It must be relevant so people hearing the name will associate it with your project in their minds, possibly for years or decades to come. Being novel will reduce the likelihood of your project being confused with other projects.

If you need to have a long name, you might want to try its initials as an acronym.

Activity

This book is full of activities. Select a project you are familiar with – preferably a future project you want to undertake. In completing the activities, you get some practice along the way while you are reading the book. You can do this as a strictly mental exercise, although there is probably more value in writing it down.

Identify a project with which you are familiar. Give the project a short, relevant, novel name. Try a few names (maybe on someone you respect) before you settle on the final one.

5.2 The Project Objective(s)

Projects may have one or many objectives, as there are often a few things to accomplish. If you can, try to keep to 3 or so objectives, otherwise you might end up losing focus or chasing your tail.

The project objective(s) should answer the question: "What do I want to achieve/avoid through doing this project?" and satisfy the answer to "Why am I doing it?"

There is a simple rule you can apply to ensure you have rigorous and complete project objectives. This is known as the SMART Model. SMART is an acronym for Specific, Measurable, Achievable, Relevant and Timeframes.

- **S**pecific — Clearly states what must be achieved.
- **M**easurable — Clearly states how success will be measured.
- **A**chievable — Is realistic in terms of effort and expenditure.
- **R**elevant — Meets the organisation's strategic plan; contributes to achievement of a significant venture.
- **T**imebound — Clearly states start and end times, and downtime if appropriate.

Of the above five components of objectives, Achievable and Relevant are not always documented, although you must ensure you consider them in writing the objective(s).

Project Objective Example – The Garden Shed

As I have no room in the garage for my gardening tools, I will do the following project:

To build a two-door garden shed that is 2 metres wide, 1.8 metres deep and 2 metres tall and has two doors on the concrete slab in my backyard. Starting this Saturday morning, and finishing by sundown Sunday.

I am using a kit and have done this once before, so do not expect any major problems.

Explanation of Example:

Specific	... build a garden shed ...
Measurable	... that is 2 metres wide, 1.8 metres deep and 2 metres tall and has two doors on the concrete slab in my backyard ...
Achievable	... (I am using a kit and have done this once before) ...
Relevant	... (I have no room in the garage for my gardening tools)...
Timebound	... starting this Saturday morning, and finishing by sundown Sunday.

The Ultimate Objective

In addition to the Project Objective, in many situations there is an Ultimate Objective. The Ultimate Objective is the project's purpose. In the case of the building of the Chunnel (the tunnel beneath the English Channel), the Project Objective involved digging 3 long tunnels, lining them with concrete and laying railway tracks. However, the Ultimate Objective was linking England with the Continent of Europe, a far larger undertaking. For some people the Ultimate Objective may have been to improve links between the United Kingdom and the European Union.

Be sure to know and understand the Ultimate Objective. (This is also sometimes called 'the venture'.)

How to Plan Small Projects

Activity

Take a sheet of paper and write the letters SMART down the left side. Write the objective on the right side of your page. Depending on the nature of the project, you might need to write a few of these.

Write the Ultimate Objective(s) of the project.

Project Deliverables & Scope

By examining your project objectives you should be able to identify a small number of 'project deliverables', or 'outputs'. These are tangible things you will create or achieve during or by the end of the project.

The 'scope' of the project is the set of deliverables. Either stated or implied, the things that will not be delivered are 'out of scope'.

For example, a person quoting to paint a house may state that the walls and eaves are included in the price, but that the gutters and downpipes are 'out of scope' as they already have a long-life paint.

Make sure you are very clear on the scope.

Activity

Draw a line down the middle of a page to make two columns. Label the left column 'in scope' and the right 'out of scope'. List your deliverables in the left column and some things you will not deliver in the right.

Challenge the Project – Ask Why?

This is a good time to ask "why am I doing this?", and to make sure that your objectives and deliverables are realistic and relevant.

5.3 The Project Client

You need to know who you are doing the project for, and what involvement that person or persons may need to have in order for the project to succeed. Enlightened project managers seek 'buy-in' ('agreement' regarding significant decisions) and 'sign-off'. In some cases, you are the client. That is, you are doing the project for yourself. If that is the case, this topic needs little attention.

Although you can generate some 'buy-in' by promoting the project to the client, and encouraging their involvement, be very cautious if you have to work too hard at this. It is better to have no project than a project with no client.

There will be many important decisions in the life of a project. Running decisions past the client can avoid costly rework and the loss of the client's confidence. If a decision is needed, but there are no compelling reasons to go one way or another, the client can be invited to make a decisions with minimal risk to the project. Where there is risk to the project of a poor decision, you may need to spend considerable time promoting your preferred outcome.

Client Signoff

Sign-off is the approval of the client. This may be a verbal or written approval. Obviously a written approval carries more 'weight', and is more likely to be legally binding.

Rather than leaving this to the end of the project, it is sensible to seek approval at regular intervals – commencing with the Project Objective or the Project Definition; or maybe even commencing with approval to spend time writing the Project Objective and the Project Definition.

Activity

Write down the name of the client. Describe what you know about the client that is relevant to the project. List the project activities in which you will involve the client.

How to Plan Small Projects

If you are the client, you may have covered this step while writing your project objectives and deliverables.

Bad Clients

Not all clients are created equal. Sadly some clients are not committed to the project – they may have other priorities, or even see the failure of the project as desirable. They may move rapidly between demonstrating a passionate commitment to the project and completely ignore its existence.

If you have a bad client you should make a choice – to stay and make the best of the situation, or to go. If you choose to stay, you may be able to promote the project to the extent that it becomes a priority again; but if you do, you should not assume this will stay a priority without constant attention from you. You may be able to promote the project to someone else, perhaps securing their commitment and supplanting the bad client with a good one. You may just find that you are hung out to dry.

5.4 Project Activities

This is really just a cursory look at what needs to be done on the project. You will plan what needs to be done in much more detail in the Project Schedule.

In planning for the project, it is useful to have a broad understanding of what will be done, and to continue to build on this understanding as your plans progress. If you start this now, when you come to write the Project Schedule, you will already have a lot of the content of the schedule. Your list of activities may be quite basic, or extremely thorough. Either way, keep in mind, these are the activities we expect to accomplish. They are not necessarily all of the ones we will accomplish.

Activity

Write a list of project activities that includes (a) the really important activities; (b) what you need to do to get the project started; and (c) what you will need to do to get it finished. (Keep in mind your Project Objective.)

Lead Time

'Lead time' is the time we have before something is to happen. In project planning lead time is used to prepare for the project. When we talk about lead time, some people persist in saying, 'let's get on with it'. What they mean is 'I think I know what needs to be done; and I can't be bothered taking the time to write it down; check whether it is realistic; and make sure the other people involved know what I know'.

Take the time you need to plan properly before you start. If you are not sure how much time to allow, take a guess and double it.

5.5 Project Team

The people needed result directly from the Project Activities. You need to identify 'project roles' and match 'available people' to these.

Identifying project roles involves grouping project activities into jobs, and identifying the required skills. When the available people do not have the required skills, you can work on building skills; expand the pool of available people; and/or turn away people who are unlikely to make a worthwhile contribution.

Some useful things to know about people include skills, preferences, availability and cost.

We need to know their 'skills' so we can determine whether they can do the job. People will often work harder on tasks for which they have a 'preference'. 'Availability' is critical, as progressing the project efficiently involves keeping to a schedule of work. In some cases this will need to be altered to accommodate availability. In many cases there will be a 'cost'. You need to add the cost to your budget (see Project Budget below).

Three intangible factors that can have a huge impact on project success are: ability to work in a team environment; willingness/ability to learn; and ability to live with uncertainty.

Teams

The 'ability to work in a team environment' is also a deal-breaker. The project environment is often a pressure cooker environment. As my friend Cindy Plant says, lone wolves and solitary wombats are unlikely to thrive.

Selection for willingness/ability to learn and ability to work in a team environment is a difficult task, but far easier than getting people who do not have these attributes to work cooperatively on you project.

Learning

'Willingness/ability to learn' is often critical on projects, as it is far easier to move people between tasks than to move people into and out of the project, and possibly back into the project later. Instead we try to do as much as possible with the people we have.

Uncertainty

Projects often involve a lot of uncertainty. Your ability, and the ability of your team members, to tolerate uncertainty can impact on project success. Seek out people who can tolerate uncertainty.

Activity

Write the names of the people who will participate in the project. (Some people may not yet exist. In their case give a name to their 'role'.) Put the names into a table with column headings like: Skills; Preferences; Availability; Cost. Fill in these columns.

The Lichtig Score (Project Teams)

Will Lichtig is an attorney who is concerned about construction projects' failure to keep up with productivity increases elsewhere in the economy, and the failure to keep people safe. He calls projects 'temporary social organisations', and proposes a project management equivalent of the newborn babies' Apgar score.

Will examines five aspects of projects: collaborative planning; reliable promising; unaccounted-for foreseeable issues; safety; and project mood. He gives a rating of 0, 1 or 2 on each aspect.

(Lichtig, W. 2007 "Projects as Patients: What Can We Learn from the Medical Profession," *Practice Management Digest*, The American Institute of Architects, Fall 2007.)

5.6 Project Budget

There are lots of different kinds of costs – including fixed and variable costs; and operational and capital costs. In planning costs for small projects, I like to distinguish between 'cumulative' and 'lump-sum' costs.

Cumulative costs are those that increase as you do more, or as tasks take longer. For example, when you are paying a contractor an hourly rate.

Lump sum costs are those that will cost a particular amount. For example, when you have a quote from an electrician for lighting and power points.

Lump sums can vary, but generally only under particular recognisable circumstances, such as when we later ask the electrician to add a new safety switch to the fuse box. In this case the electrician will have a legitimate reason to ask for more money.

Wrapped up in the need to budget is the need for a source of funds. Identifying and making firm friends (or at least developing a grudging mutual respect) with the person through whom you obtain the funds is very important.

Contingency

Heraclitus (c. 535-475 BCE) told us to 'expect the unexpected'. This is especially relevant on projects.

You also need to ensure that you can afford the unexpected – such as the people you are paying an hourly rate taking longer than planned; or doing things that are in the project scope, but that you left out of the budget. You can do this by going back to the source of the project funds and asking for more money. Alternatively, while planning you can add a contingency figure to the figures in your budget. This is to cover for small additional costs.

A project managers' rule of thumb is to add 10% contingency.

10% gives you a buffer for some basic errors in estimating.

You may need more than a 10% contingency. For example, if a key cost is likely to rise substantially during the life of the project; or due to the newness of what you are doing you are not confident in your estimates of time and cost. In this case consider adding more contingency. But remember, a high contingency may stand out and need to be justified. A really high contingency may prevent the project from going ahead (which may even be the best outcome).

Microsoft Excel™ (or another spreadsheet program) is a good place to record your budget, although you can equally use a pen and paper (and calculator if needed).

Activity

Identify what costs you will have, estimate how much they will be, and distinguish between cumulative and lump-sum costs. Then add 10% to see the impact of a modest contingency.

5.7 Project End

My good friend Cindy Plant says this is one of her favourite things about projects. Even if they are difficult, they will not go forever – like childbirth, they end and hopefully deliver something that brings joy.

At this point in your planning you may have a deadline for the project – a 'must finish on' date. In the next section you will develop a schedule, giving you a better idea of when the project should finish.

If you do not have a fixed deadline, you should be coy about sharing when you expect the project to finish.

Even when you have a finish date, if you are going to be presenting it to people who would see it as a commitment, consider adding some time. This is another kind of contingency – in this case a time contingency as opposed to a cost contingency.

Projects seldom finish early. We often identify tasks 'along the way', or decide to do more than we had planned. (This is called 'scope creep' and is considered a no-no in sophisticated project management circles. Realistically if we see that something more should be done and it is unlikely to have severe consequences, we may do it.)

Activity

If you have a deadline, write it down. If not, have a guess, so you can see how close you are when you write the schedule, and when you finish the project.

5.8 The Project Name (again)

At this point you should go back to your project name and have a good, hard look at it. Now that you know so much more about the project, the name may have changed completely, or you may be able to make it more accurate and descriptive.

6. The Project Schedule

You should have at least a basic schedule before the project starts. In its most basic form the Project Schedule is a series of activities with due dates.

Task	Due Date
1. Prepare work site.	9:00
2. Review shed blueprint/plans.	9:15
3. Erect walls.	10:45
Etc.	

More detail can include:

- Identifying stages of the project (also known as phases).
- Breaking big tasks down into smaller tasks.
- 'Linking' tasks that are related to each other.
- Adding expected durations for activities.
- Assigning people and other resources to the activities.
- Identifying milestones (really important things).

Various tools can be used, such as a large piece of paper (lined or unlined); a spreadsheet in Excel™ or similar; or a table in Word™. The layout on the following page is a table in Word™:

How to Plan Small Projects

A Simple Template for a Project Schedule

Project/Initiative:						
Completion Date:		Project Manager:				
Project Objectives:		Project Deliverables:				
Tasks	Work Effort (hours)	Duration (days)	People	Materials/Tools/ Equipment	Deadline (If applicable)

How to Plan Small Projects

6.1 Create the Project Schedule

To create your Project Schedule, do the following tasks (leaving out any which are overkill for your situation). Take breaks frequently.

1. Brainstorm all the possible project tasks. (A pad of Post-it Notes™ and a whiteboard/clear table can be handy for this.)

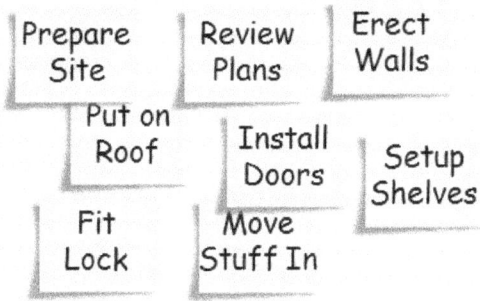

2. Consider where/how the project will start and finish, and add any extra tasks to your list.
3. Consider any external influences on the project, and add them in.
4. Decide whether there are major stages, and split the tasks into the stages. (Group the Post-it Notes™.)
5. Sequence the tasks roughly in the order in which they should happen. (Put the Post-it Notes™ in order, from left to right with tasks that can be done at the same time in parallel.)

23.

How to Plan Small Projects

6. If you have a final deadline, write it against the last task.
7. Add people and materials/tools/equipment for each task.
8. Decide how many hours of work effort each task should need; and what duration in days should take to get it done.

   (For example, the work effort to paint a room might be only 5 hours, but between tea breaks and paint drying, the duration may be 2 days.)
9. Underline or bold any really, really important tasks.
10. Show it to someone else, and explain it to them.
    (Only make changes that improve the schedule.)

Note: If all you need is a basic schedule, just do steps 1, 5 and 8.

Activity

Create a Project Schedule. If you can, ask for someone else's input – two heads can be better than one.

Assessing Quality

You should be assessing the 'quality' of the project's performance. This often involves scrutinising project deliverables as they are developed. When this is the case, these 'review' steps need to be incorporated into the project activities, to ensure they are not overlooked.

6.2 Enough or More Needed?

The next topic is about adding more details to your Project Definition, depending on the size and complexity of your project, these may not be necessary. Read the questions on the next page if you are not sure. If you are ready to start now, all the best with your project. If not, keep reading…

7. A More Comprehensive Project Definition

You can add any or all of the following to the Project Definition to make it even more comprehensive.

11. How am I going to keep track and how will I report project status?	Project Monitoring & Reporting
12. Does my organisation have the will and the capacity, to complete the project?	Organisational Motivation & Organisational Capacity
13. Who is important to the project, and why?	Stakeholder Analysis
14. Where will the project be undertaken, and where is the best place/space?	Project Location
15. How can the resources be secured by the project?	Securing & Keeping Resources
16. What are the known risks and issues and how will I address them?	Project Risks & Issues

You are unlikely to include all of these elements in Project Definitions. So it is worth having a go at using all of them now, then you are more likely to use them when they are warranted. For this reason, I suggest you do the Activities in each of the topics below.

7.1 Project Monitoring & Reporting

Project monitoring can be the difference between 'on time and on budget' and 'late, costing way too much and not having warned the people affected'. So we monitor project progress closely and regularly.

Regular reporting of progress to people with an interest, including the project team, can keep you focussed on project monitoring. Even if progress reports are not required, they are a great way to promote the project if it is going well, communicate issues if it is not, and manage people's expectations.

A weekly or fortnightly progress report could include:

Title	The project name and 'Weekly (or Fortnightly) Report As At' and the date.
Current Tasks	A short list of tasks currently underway.
Project Progress	Stating what has been completed in the period just ended; and what is expected to be completed in the next period.
Variation	An explanation for how the budget, workdays and/or timelines have varied from the original plan (whether positive or negative).
Issues	A brief description of any significant issues, including the action being taken.

How to Plan Small Projects

To encourage team members to monitor their own progress, request mini-status reports. This could be an email or a jotted down note including:

Period & Date	'Weekly Report As At' and the date.
Current Activity	What they are working on right now.
Progress	An indication of when this activity will be completed.
Next	An indication of what they expect to do next.
Issues	The things that are preventing or soon to prevent the person from progressing their work.

Catastrophes

You should report catastrophes separately to the regular reporting cycle. Catastrophes are often too urgent to wait for the next status report. These can be written in the following way:
- What the catastrophe is.
- What impact it could/will/has had on the project.
- What could be done to resolve it (multiple alternatives).
- What alternative is recommended by the person raising the issue (including why and what it will cost – in both dollars and time).

Activity

For the project you have been working on, write down how you plan to monitor work performance and project progress. Keep your approach simple, as it is easy to overdo this activity on small projects.

7.2 Organisational Commitment & Capacity

An ongoing commitment to the project is critical. The organisation needs to be motivated to encourage and support the project. This includes willingness to promote the project, to fund the project, and to give their time to ensuring the success of the project.

Commitment has a tendency to wane, especially for long projects. If commitment is half-hearted at the start of the project, it is likely to get worse before it gets better. Sometimes the project manager needs to remind the organisation of its commitment. You cannot force commitment, but you can encourage it.

The organisation must also have the capacity to complete the project. This capacity may be in-house, or in some cases 'brought in' from outside in the form of outsourcing or a partnership. Capacity is about having the skills, resources and processes to undertake the project.

If you cannot secure commitment and capacity, you do not have a project.

Activity

Describe the level of commitment your organisation has for your project; and describe the skills, resources and processes (that is, capacity) required to undertake the project.

7.3 Stakeholder Analysis

Stakeholders are generally individuals or groups with an interest in the project and hopefully an interest in the project's success. They may include:
- The people who will use the outcomes of the project.
- The project sponsor (the source of funds).
- Your customers or clients.
- Influential suppliers.
- Your boss, and your boss's boss.

Some of these may be split up or combined. For example, the client may include 'the people who will use the project outcomes' and 'the project sponsor'.

You need to know the following:

(Level of) Influence	How much influence they have over your project – High, Medium or Low.
Their Expectations (of the Project)	What they expect the project to achieve.
How They Will be Involved (in the Project)	By involving stakeholders we can often convert an interest in the project into good project outcomes.

Activity

Draw up a table with headings: Stakeholder; Level of Influence; Their Expectations; How They Will be Involved. Add the stakeholders down the left column. Then fill in the details for the stakeholders with High influence.

7.4 Project Location

Project location can provide advantages and disadvantages.

At the very least, based on the location you may be able to identify some important considerations for the project, including risks, enablers of project success, proximity to the client, access to technical support and more. For example, if the project involves collecting sea water samples, proximity to the ocean may be important.

Proximity of members of the project team is also important. Professor Thomas J. Allen of MIT is frequently cited as stating that people working more than 15 metres apart are unlikely to collaborate more than once a week. So if people who need to work together are more than 15 metres apart, you should take extra effort to get them to work together. Or even better, get people to co-locate.

Activity

Identify the location(s) at which the project will be done. Note any characteristics of the location that will help or hinder the project.

7.5 Securing & Keeping Resources

This section involves documenting the project's strategy for securing the resources that will be needed on the project. This is generally only required in environments where the required resources are scarce or distant from the project location.

In a hierarchical organisation often the path to securing resources is to get the commitment of the manager with control of the resources you need.

In a social environment – from moving house to raising a barn – you may need to cater. If so, make sure you provide the best food and beverages the project can afford.

Motivating People

Motivation is critical. Some things that can assist in motivating people include:
- Involving them in writing the plan.
- Clear communication of goals and direction.
- Agreement with the goals and direction.
- Good interpersonal relationships on the team.
- Regular updates of progress towards goals.
- Opportunity to develop new skills.
- Recognition of a good effort.
- The example of a committed work ethic (set by you).

Activity

State how you will get and hold onto critical project resources.

7.6 Project Risks & Issues

Risks and issues are two different things, but they can often be recorded together. This is because they have an important aspect in common – both mean problems for the project. Risks are potential problems; and issues are actual problems. Although in many cases this distinction is not particularly useful.

Project managers should record known risks and issues. Some project managers seem to think this is all that needs to be done. In fact, you will need to decide what needs to be done about them, and put what needs to be done into the project schedule.

Note: For large and complex projects, more details are recorded, and a more rigorous and analytical process is followed in managing risks and issues.

Problems

37signals, a web design company, in their book *Getting Real*, instruct the project manager not to deal with problems before they are problems.

When you fly on connecting flights there is a risk that due to a delay you will miss the connection. It would be unusual to book an extra ('Plan B') flight in case of delay.

Activity

Write a list of all of the issues/risks that you can think of. Put an asterisk next to the most important ones. For the most important ones write down what you have done or are going to do about them.

7.7 Are You Finished Yet?

If you have done some or all of the activities in this chapter, you have an enhanced Project Definition.

It really is now time to get started on your project. For habitual procrastinators, you can go back to the beginning and refine your plan further. For the rest of you, all the best with your project.

Project Plan Template

(A Word™ version is available in Resources > How to Plan Small Projects at www.performancepeople.com.au.)

Project Plan

Project Definition

Project Name
What to call the project?

Project Objective
What do I want to achieve?

The Ultimate Objective
Why am I doing the project? (It's ultimate purpose.)

Project Deliverables (& Scope)

What are the tangible things I will do/create?	What is 'out of scope'?

How to Plan Small Projects

Project Client
Who am I doing it for?

Project Activities

How am I going to start?	What will I do along the way?	How am I going to finish?

Project Team
Who else will be doing the project?

Project Budget
What should the project cost?

Project End
How soon do I need to/expect to finish?

(Note: Remember to check your Project Name.)

35.

How to Plan Small Projects

Project Schedule

Tasks	Work (hrs)	Duration (days)	People/Materials/ Tools/Equipment	Due Date
1.				
2.				
3.				
4.				
5.				
6.				
7.				
8.				
9.				
10.				
11.				
12.				
13.				
14.				
15.				

A More Comprehensive Project Definition

Project Monitoring & Reporting
How am I going to keep track and how will I report project status?

Organisational Motivation & Organisational Capacity
Does my organisation have the will and the capacity, to complete the project?

Stakeholder Analysis
Who is important to the project, and why?

Stake-holder	(Level of) Influence	Their Expectations	How They Will be Involved

Project Location

Where will the project be undertaken, and where is the best place/space?

Securing & Keeping Resources

How can the resources be secured by the project?

Project Risks & Issues

What are the known risks and issues, and how will I address them?

Known Risk/Issue	Action/Response

8. Endnote: An Explanation

This book started as an experimental blog. It failed spectacularly (well, spectacularly for me, as I expected it to be something that it wasn't).

The blog introduction said:

Hi,

I have been planning to write a book called "How to Manage Small Projects", with a catchy but as yet not invented phrase to follow the title. The book has been in me for about a decade now.

I went to a workshop on how to write a book in the middle of this year (2007), which was actually about how to publish a book – which was lucky as I know a fair bit about writing, but little about publishing. Full of vim and vigour I finished* a plan for the book in no time at all (August 2007) – mostly on my PDA while sitting at the school waiting for the bell to release my children – I correctly figured that the limitations of the teeny-tiny keyboard would keep my plan short and to the point.

Now that the plan has sat for about two months, it is time to push on. This blog is my method of stringing out the whole process a bit further, as I am a bit scared of the self-publishing process. Also, as I have been trying to convince my Dad to blog, this is a good opportunity to lead by example.

* For 'finished', read 'decided I'd identified enough topics to fill a book'.

Now it is September 2010. The blog is long abandoned, and the book is done. I hope that you have enjoyed it, and that your projects are 'on target and on time'.

...Geoff Higgins

Acknowledgements

I'd like to thank Ricki Jeffery for planting the seed.

I would also like to thank my good friends Cindy and Michael Plant and Douglas Elsmore for lively discussions about the management of projects. And to especially thank Cindy for her close review of the manuscript and excellent advice.

I would like to thank Joan James, Mary Lancaster and Neil Perry of Andersen Consulting as we were then (now Accenture) for coaching me in the arcane art of project management.

I would also like to thank Seth Godin for exhorting me (not personally, but by blog) to publish and be damned; Marelisa Fabrega (at www.squidoo.com) for her publishing advice; and Robyn Henderson for an inspiring workshop in 2007.

Finally, I would like to thank my family – Peta-Anne, for her editing and support and for being the best business partner ever; and Emma, Eloise and Charlotte for their forbearance of a father who is often there in body, but less often in mind.

www.ingramcontent.com/pod-product-compliance
Lightning Source LLC
Chambersburg PA
CBHW031218090426
42736CB00009B/975